50 Plant-Powered Plates Recipes for Home

By: Kelly Johnson

Table of Contents

- Chickpea Salad Sandwich
- Quinoa-Stuffed Bell Peppers
- Sweet Potato and Black Bean Tacos
- Zucchini Noodles with Avocado Sauce
- Lentil Bolognese
- Cauliflower Curry with Spinach
- Vegan Mushroom Stroganoff
- Mediterranean Quinoa Bowl
- Thai Peanut Sweet Potato Buddha Bowl
- Spaghetti Squash with Marinara
- Roasted Beet and Citrus Salad
- Coconut Chickpea Stew
- Avocado Toast with Cherry Tomatoes
- Vegan Chili with Kidney Beans
- Spinach and Mushroom Stuffed Portobellos
- Grilled Vegetable Skewers
- Lentil and Vegetable Shepherd's Pie
- Chia Seed Pudding with Almond Milk
- Butternut Squash Risotto
- Cauliflower Tacos with Lime Crema
- Creamy Vegan Mushroom Soup
- Rainbow Vegetable Stir-Fry
- Sweet Potato and Chickpea Buddha Bowl
- Black Bean and Quinoa Salad
- Roasted Garlic Hummus
- Apple and Walnut Salad
- Vegan Pad Thai with Tofu
- Stuffed Acorn Squash with Quinoa
- Baked Falafel with Tahini Sauce
- Zesty Lime Rice with Beans
- Kale and Quinoa Salad
- Coconut Rice with Mango
- Vegan Stuffed Cabbage Rolls
- Chickpea and Spinach Stew
- Grilled Eggplant with Tahini Drizzle

- Vegan Lentil Tacos
- Savory Oatmeal with Spinach and Avocado
- Cucumber and Avocado Sushi Rolls
- Maple Glazed Brussels Sprouts
- Spicy Roasted Chickpeas
- Cauliflower Fried Rice
- Miso Soup with Tofu and Seaweed
- Vegan Chocolate Avocado Pudding
- Berry and Spinach Smoothie Bowl
- Curried Carrot and Apple Soup
- Quinoa and Black Bean Burger
- Green Goddess Salad
- Roasted Tomato and Basil Pasta
- Plant-Based Sushi with Vegetables
- Chocolate Chia Seed Energy Bites

Chickpea Salad Sandwich

Ingredients

- 1 can (15 oz) chickpeas, rinsed and drained
- 1/4 cup mayonnaise or vegan mayo
- 1 tablespoon Dijon mustard
- 1/4 cup celery, diced
- 1/4 cup red onion, diced
- Salt and pepper to taste
- Whole grain bread or wraps
- Lettuce and tomato (for serving)

Instructions

1. **Mash Chickpeas:**
   - In a bowl, mash chickpeas with a fork, leaving some chunks for texture.
2. **Mix Ingredients:**
   - Stir in mayonnaise, Dijon mustard, celery, red onion, salt, and pepper until well combined.
3. **Assemble Sandwich:**
   - Spread the chickpea mixture on bread or wraps and top with lettuce and tomato.
4. **Serve:**
   - Cut in half and enjoy!

Quinoa-Stuffed Bell Peppers

Ingredients

- 4 bell peppers, halved and seeds removed
- 1 cup cooked quinoa
- 1 can (15 oz) black beans, rinsed and drained
- 1 cup corn (fresh, frozen, or canned)
- 1 teaspoon cumin
- 1 teaspoon chili powder
- Salt and pepper to taste
- 1 cup salsa

Instructions

1. **Preheat the Oven:**
   - Preheat your oven to 375°F (190°C).
2. **Mix Filling:**
   - In a bowl, combine cooked quinoa, black beans, corn, cumin, chili powder, salt, pepper, and salsa.
3. **Stuff Peppers:**
   - Fill each bell pepper half with the quinoa mixture and place them in a baking dish.
4. **Bake:**
   - Cover with foil and bake for 30-35 minutes until peppers are tender.
5. **Serve:**
   - Enjoy warm, optionally topped with avocado or cheese.

Sweet Potato and Black Bean Tacos

Ingredients

- 2 medium sweet potatoes, peeled and diced
- 1 can (15 oz) black beans, rinsed and drained
- 1 teaspoon cumin
- 1 teaspoon paprika
- Salt and pepper to taste
- Corn or flour tortillas
- Toppings: avocado, cilantro, lime, salsa

Instructions

1. **Cook Sweet Potatoes:**
   - In a pot, boil sweet potatoes until tender, about 10-15 minutes. Drain and mash slightly.
2. **Mix Ingredients:**
   - Stir in black beans, cumin, paprika, salt, and pepper.
3. **Assemble Tacos:**
   - Warm tortillas and fill with the sweet potato mixture.
4. **Serve:**
   - Top with avocado, cilantro, lime juice, and salsa.

Zucchini Noodles with Avocado Sauce

Ingredients

- 2 medium zucchinis, spiralized
- 1 ripe avocado
- 1 clove garlic
- 2 tablespoons lemon juice
- 1/4 cup fresh basil
- Salt and pepper to taste
- Cherry tomatoes (for garnish)

Instructions

1. **Make Avocado Sauce:**
    - In a blender, combine avocado, garlic, lemon juice, basil, salt, and pepper. Blend until smooth.
2. **Sauté Zoodles:**
    - In a skillet, lightly sauté zucchini noodles for 2-3 minutes until just tender.
3. **Combine:**
    - Toss zucchini noodles with avocado sauce until well coated.
4. **Serve:**
    - Top with cherry tomatoes and enjoy!

Lentil Bolognese

Ingredients

- 1 cup lentils (brown or green), rinsed
- 1 onion, diced
- 2 carrots, diced
- 2 celery stalks, diced
- 2 cloves garlic, minced
- 1 can (28 oz) crushed tomatoes
- 1 teaspoon dried oregano
- 1 teaspoon basil
- Salt and pepper to taste
- Pasta of choice

Instructions

1. **Cook Lentils:**
    - In a pot, combine lentils with 3 cups of water. Bring to a boil, reduce heat, and simmer for 20-25 minutes until tender.
2. **Sauté Vegetables:**
    - In a skillet, sauté onion, carrots, celery, and garlic until soft.
3. **Combine:**
    - Add crushed tomatoes, cooked lentils, oregano, basil, salt, and pepper. Simmer for 15 minutes.
4. **Serve:**
    - Serve over pasta of choice.

Cauliflower Curry with Spinach

Ingredients

- 1 head cauliflower, cut into florets
- 2 cups fresh spinach
- 1 can (14 oz) coconut milk
- 2 tablespoons curry powder
- 1 onion, diced
- 2 cloves garlic, minced
- Salt and pepper to taste
- Cooked rice (for serving)

Instructions

1. **Sauté Onion and Garlic:**
   - In a pot, sauté onion and garlic until soft.
2. **Add Cauliflower:**
   - Stir in cauliflower and curry powder, cooking for a few minutes.
3. **Add Coconut Milk:**
   - Pour in coconut milk and simmer for 15 minutes until cauliflower is tender.
4. **Stir in Spinach:**
   - Add spinach and cook until wilted. Season with salt and pepper.
5. **Serve:**
   - Serve over cooked rice.

Vegan Mushroom Stroganoff

Ingredients

- 8 oz mushrooms, sliced
- 1 onion, diced
- 2 cloves garlic, minced
- 1 cup vegetable broth
- 1 cup coconut milk or cashew cream
- 1 tablespoon soy sauce
- 1 teaspoon paprika
- Salt and pepper to taste
- Pasta or rice (for serving)

Instructions

1. **Sauté Vegetables:**
    - In a skillet, sauté mushrooms, onion, and garlic until tender.
2. **Add Broth and Cream:**
    - Stir in vegetable broth, coconut milk, soy sauce, and paprika. Simmer for 10 minutes.
3. **Season:**
    - Season with salt and pepper.
4. **Serve:**
    - Serve over pasta or rice.

Mediterranean Quinoa Bowl

Ingredients

- 1 cup cooked quinoa
- 1 cup cherry tomatoes, halved
- 1 cucumber, diced
- 1/4 cup Kalamata olives, sliced
- 1/4 cup feta cheese (optional)
- 2 tablespoons olive oil
- Juice of 1 lemon
- Salt and pepper to taste
- Fresh parsley (for garnish)

Instructions

1. **Combine Ingredients:**
    - In a large bowl, mix cooked quinoa, cherry tomatoes, cucumber, olives, and feta cheese (if using).
2. **Dress Salad:**
    - Drizzle with olive oil, lemon juice, salt, and pepper. Toss gently.
3. **Serve:**
    - Garnish with fresh parsley and enjoy!

Enjoy your delicious meals!

Thai Peanut Sweet Potato Buddha Bowl

Ingredients

- 2 medium sweet potatoes, diced
- 1 cup cooked quinoa
- 1 cup broccoli florets
- 1 cup shredded carrots
- 1/2 cup red cabbage, shredded
- 1/4 cup peanut butter
- 2 tablespoons soy sauce
- 1 tablespoon lime juice
- 1 teaspoon maple syrup (optional)
- Chopped peanuts and cilantro (for garnish)

Instructions

1. **Roast Sweet Potatoes:**
    - Preheat your oven to 400°F (200°C). Toss diced sweet potatoes with olive oil, salt, and pepper. Roast for 25-30 minutes until tender.
2. **Steam Broccoli:**
    - Steam broccoli florets for about 5 minutes until bright green and tender.
3. **Make Peanut Sauce:**
    - In a bowl, whisk together peanut butter, soy sauce, lime juice, and maple syrup until smooth. Add a little water to thin if necessary.
4. **Assemble Bowls:**
    - In bowls, layer quinoa, roasted sweet potatoes, broccoli, carrots, and cabbage. Drizzle with peanut sauce.
5. **Serve:**
    - Top with chopped peanuts and cilantro.

Spaghetti Squash with Marinara

Ingredients

- 1 medium spaghetti squash
- 2 cups marinara sauce
- 1 tablespoon olive oil
- Salt and pepper to taste
- Fresh basil (for garnish)

Instructions

1. **Cook Spaghetti Squash:**
   - Preheat the oven to 400°F (200°C). Cut the spaghetti squash in half, scoop out the seeds, and drizzle with olive oil, salt, and pepper. Place cut side down on a baking sheet and bake for 30-40 minutes until tender.
2. **Prepare Marinara:**
   - While the squash is cooking, heat marinara sauce in a saucepan over medium heat.
3. **Shred Squash:**
   - Once the squash is cooked, use a fork to shred the flesh into spaghetti-like strands.
4. **Combine:**
   - Mix shredded squash with marinara sauce.
5. **Serve:**
   - Garnish with fresh basil and enjoy!

Roasted Beet and Citrus Salad

Ingredients

- 2 medium beets, roasted and diced
- 2 cups mixed greens
- 1 orange, segmented
- 1/4 cup feta cheese (optional)
- 2 tablespoons olive oil
- 1 tablespoon balsamic vinegar
- Salt and pepper to taste

Instructions

1. **Roast Beets:**
   - Preheat your oven to 400°F (200°C). Wrap beets in foil and roast for about 45-60 minutes until tender. Let cool, then peel and dice.
2. **Assemble Salad:**
   - In a large bowl, combine mixed greens, roasted beets, orange segments, and feta cheese (if using).
3. **Dress Salad:**
   - Drizzle with olive oil, balsamic vinegar, salt, and pepper. Toss gently.
4. **Serve:**
   - Enjoy as a refreshing side or light main dish.

Coconut Chickpea Stew

Ingredients

- 1 can (15 oz) chickpeas, rinsed and drained
- 1 can (14 oz) coconut milk
- 1 can (14 oz) diced tomatoes
- 1 onion, diced
- 2 cloves garlic, minced
- 1 tablespoon curry powder
- 2 cups spinach
- Salt and pepper to taste

Instructions

1. **Sauté Onions and Garlic:**
    - In a pot, sauté onion and garlic until softened.
2. **Add Ingredients:**
    - Stir in chickpeas, coconut milk, diced tomatoes, curry powder, salt, and pepper. Bring to a simmer.
3. **Add Spinach:**
    - Stir in spinach and cook until wilted.
4. **Serve:**
    - Enjoy warm, optionally with rice or bread.

Avocado Toast with Cherry Tomatoes

Ingredients

- 2 slices whole grain bread
- 1 ripe avocado
- 1 cup cherry tomatoes, halved
- Salt and pepper to taste
- Red pepper flakes (optional)
- Fresh basil (for garnish)

Instructions

1. **Toast Bread:**
   - Toast the slices of whole grain bread until golden.
2. **Prepare Avocado:**
   - In a bowl, mash avocado and season with salt and pepper.
3. **Assemble Toast:**
   - Spread mashed avocado on toasted bread, top with halved cherry tomatoes, and sprinkle with red pepper flakes.
4. **Serve:**
   - Garnish with fresh basil and enjoy!

Vegan Chili with Kidney Beans

Ingredients

- 1 can (15 oz) kidney beans, rinsed and drained
- 1 can (15 oz) black beans, rinsed and drained
- 1 can (28 oz) crushed tomatoes
- 1 onion, diced
- 2 cloves garlic, minced
- 1 bell pepper, diced
- 2 tablespoons chili powder
- 1 teaspoon cumin
- Salt and pepper to taste

Instructions

1. **Sauté Vegetables:**
    - In a pot, sauté onion, garlic, and bell pepper until softened.
2. **Add Remaining Ingredients:**
    - Stir in kidney beans, black beans, crushed tomatoes, chili powder, cumin, salt, and pepper. Bring to a simmer.
3. **Cook:**
    - Let simmer for 20-30 minutes, stirring occasionally.
4. **Serve:**
    - Enjoy warm, optionally with toppings like avocado or cilantro.

Spinach and Mushroom Stuffed Portobellos

Ingredients

- 4 large portobello mushrooms, stems removed
- 2 cups spinach, chopped
- 1 cup mushrooms, diced
- 1/2 cup breadcrumbs
- 1/4 cup nutritional yeast (optional)
- 2 cloves garlic, minced
- Salt and pepper to taste
- Olive oil for drizzling

Instructions

1. **Preheat the Oven:**
   - Preheat your oven to 375°F (190°C).
2. **Sauté Filling:**
   - In a skillet, sauté diced mushrooms and garlic until soft. Add spinach and cook until wilted. Remove from heat and mix in breadcrumbs and nutritional yeast (if using).
3. **Stuff Mushrooms:**
   - Place portobello caps on a baking sheet, fill each with the spinach mixture, and drizzle with olive oil.
4. **Bake:**
   - Bake for 20-25 minutes until mushrooms are tender.
5. **Serve:**
   - Enjoy warm as a main dish.

Grilled Vegetable Skewers

Ingredients

- 1 zucchini, sliced
- 1 bell pepper, cut into chunks
- 1 red onion, cut into chunks
- 1 cup cherry tomatoes
- 2 tablespoons olive oil
- Salt and pepper to taste
- Fresh herbs (for garnish)

Instructions

1. **Prepare Vegetables:**
    - In a bowl, toss zucchini, bell pepper, onion, and cherry tomatoes with olive oil, salt, and pepper.
2. **Skewer Vegetables:**
    - Thread the vegetables onto skewers.
3. **Grill:**
    - Preheat the grill to medium-high heat. Grill skewers for about 10-15 minutes, turning occasionally, until tender and charred.
4. **Serve:**
    - Garnish with fresh herbs and enjoy!

Enjoy your delicious meals!

Lentil and Vegetable Shepherd's Pie

Ingredients

- 1 cup lentils (green or brown), rinsed
- 2 cups vegetable broth
- 1 onion, diced
- 2 carrots, diced
- 2 celery stalks, diced
- 2 cloves garlic, minced
- 1 cup frozen peas
- 2 tablespoons tomato paste
- 1 teaspoon dried thyme
- 4 cups mashed potatoes (prepared ahead)
- Salt and pepper to taste

Instructions

1. **Cook Lentils:**
   - In a pot, combine lentils and vegetable broth. Bring to a boil, then reduce heat and simmer until lentils are tender, about 25-30 minutes.
2. **Sauté Vegetables:**
   - In a skillet, sauté onion, carrots, celery, and garlic until soft. Stir in cooked lentils, peas, tomato paste, thyme, salt, and pepper.
3. **Assemble Pie:**
   - Preheat the oven to 400°F (200°C). Transfer the lentil mixture to a baking dish and spread mashed potatoes on top.
4. **Bake:**
   - Bake for 20-25 minutes until the top is golden.
5. **Serve:**
   - Enjoy warm!

Chia Seed Pudding with Almond Milk

Ingredients

- 1/4 cup chia seeds
- 1 cup almond milk (or milk of choice)
- 1 tablespoon maple syrup (optional)
- 1/2 teaspoon vanilla extract
- Fresh fruit and nuts for topping

Instructions

1. **Mix Ingredients:**
    - In a bowl, whisk together chia seeds, almond milk, maple syrup, and vanilla extract.
2. **Refrigerate:**
    - Cover and refrigerate for at least 4 hours or overnight until thickened.
3. **Serve:**
    - Stir well before serving and top with fresh fruit and nuts.

Butternut Squash Risotto

Ingredients

- 1 cup Arborio rice
- 4 cups vegetable broth
- 1 cup butternut squash, diced
- 1 onion, diced
- 2 cloves garlic, minced
- 1/2 cup nutritional yeast (optional)
- 2 tablespoons olive oil
- Salt and pepper to taste
- Fresh parsley for garnish

Instructions

1. **Cook Squash:**
    - In a pot, steam or boil butternut squash until tender, about 10-15 minutes. Set aside.
2. **Sauté Onion and Garlic:**
    - In a large skillet, heat olive oil. Sauté onion and garlic until translucent.
3. **Add Rice:**
    - Stir in Arborio rice and cook for 1-2 minutes. Gradually add vegetable broth, one ladle at a time, stirring until absorbed.
4. **Add Squash:**
    - Once rice is creamy and cooked, stir in the cooked squash and nutritional yeast (if using). Season with salt and pepper.
5. **Serve:**
    - Garnish with fresh parsley.

Cauliflower Tacos with Lime Crema

Ingredients

- 1 head cauliflower, cut into florets
- 2 tablespoons olive oil
- 1 teaspoon chili powder
- Salt and pepper to taste
- Corn or flour tortillas
- 1/2 cup coconut yogurt (or sour cream)
- Juice of 1 lime
- Fresh cilantro for garnish

Instructions

1. **Preheat Oven:**
    - Preheat your oven to 425°F (220°C).
2. **Roast Cauliflower:**
    - Toss cauliflower with olive oil, chili powder, salt, and pepper. Spread on a baking sheet and roast for 25-30 minutes until tender.
3. **Make Lime Crema:**
    - In a bowl, mix coconut yogurt with lime juice, salt, and pepper.
4. **Assemble Tacos:**
    - Warm tortillas, fill with roasted cauliflower, and drizzle with lime crema.
5. **Serve:**
    - Garnish with fresh cilantro.

Creamy Vegan Mushroom Soup

Ingredients

- 8 oz mushrooms, sliced
- 1 onion, diced
- 2 cloves garlic, minced
- 4 cups vegetable broth
- 1 cup coconut milk (or cashew cream)
- 2 tablespoons nutritional yeast (optional)
- Salt and pepper to taste
- Fresh thyme for garnish

Instructions

1. **Sauté Vegetables:**
   - In a pot, sauté onion, garlic, and mushrooms until soft.
2. **Add Broth:**
   - Pour in vegetable broth and bring to a simmer. Cook for 10 minutes.
3. **Blend Soup:**
   - Use an immersion blender to blend until smooth (or blend in batches).
4. **Add Cream:**
   - Stir in coconut milk and nutritional yeast (if using). Season with salt and pepper.
5. **Serve:**
   - Garnish with fresh thyme.

Rainbow Vegetable Stir-Fry

Ingredients

- 2 cups mixed colorful vegetables (bell peppers, broccoli, carrots, etc.)
- 2 tablespoons soy sauce
- 1 tablespoon sesame oil
- 2 cloves garlic, minced
- 1 tablespoon ginger, minced
- Cooked rice or noodles (for serving)

Instructions

1. **Heat Oil:**
   - In a large skillet or wok, heat sesame oil over medium-high heat.
2. **Sauté Vegetables:**
   - Add garlic and ginger, sauté for 1 minute, then add mixed vegetables. Stir-fry for 5-7 minutes until tender-crisp.
3. **Add Sauce:**
   - Drizzle with soy sauce and toss to combine.
4. **Serve:**
   - Serve over cooked rice or noodles.

Sweet Potato and Chickpea Buddha Bowl

Ingredients

- 1 medium sweet potato, diced
- 1 can (15 oz) chickpeas, rinsed and drained
- 2 cups kale or spinach
- 2 tablespoons olive oil
- 1 teaspoon cumin
- Salt and pepper to taste
- Tahini or dressing of choice (for drizzling)

Instructions

1. **Roast Sweet Potatoes:**
   - Preheat the oven to 400°F (200°C). Toss sweet potatoes with olive oil, cumin, salt, and pepper. Roast for 25-30 minutes until tender.
2. **Sauté Chickpeas:**
   - In a skillet, heat chickpeas until warmed through. Season with salt and pepper.
3. **Prepare Greens:**
   - Sauté kale or spinach until wilted.
4. **Assemble Bowls:**
   - In bowls, layer roasted sweet potatoes, chickpeas, and greens. Drizzle with tahini or dressing.
5. **Serve:**
   - Enjoy warm!

Black Bean and Quinoa Salad

Ingredients

- 1 cup cooked quinoa
- 1 can (15 oz) black beans, rinsed and drained
- 1 cup corn (fresh, frozen, or canned)
- 1 bell pepper, diced
- 1/4 cup cilantro, chopped
- Juice of 1 lime
- Salt and pepper to taste

Instructions

1. **Combine Ingredients:**
    - In a large bowl, mix cooked quinoa, black beans, corn, bell pepper, and cilantro.
2. **Dress Salad:**
    - Drizzle with lime juice, and season with salt and pepper. Toss gently.
3. **Serve:**
    - Enjoy chilled or at room temperature.

Enjoy your delicious meals!

Roasted Garlic Hummus

Ingredients

- 1 can (15 oz) chickpeas, rinsed and drained
- 1/4 cup tahini
- 1/4 cup olive oil
- 1/4 cup lemon juice
- 1 head garlic, roasted
- Salt to taste
- Water (as needed for consistency)

Instructions

1. **Roast Garlic:**
    - Preheat the oven to 400°F (200°C). Wrap the garlic head in foil and roast for 30-35 minutes until soft.
2. **Blend Ingredients:**
    - In a food processor, combine chickpeas, tahini, olive oil, lemon juice, roasted garlic, and salt. Blend until smooth.
3. **Adjust Consistency:**
    - Add water as needed to achieve your desired consistency.
4. **Serve:**
    - Enjoy with pita bread, vegetables, or as a spread!

Apple and Walnut Salad

Ingredients

- 4 cups mixed greens
- 2 apples, sliced
- 1/2 cup walnuts, toasted
- 1/4 cup feta cheese (optional)
- 1/4 cup balsamic vinaigrette

Instructions

1. **Assemble Salad:**
    - In a large bowl, combine mixed greens, sliced apples, toasted walnuts, and feta cheese (if using).
2. **Dress Salad:**
    - Drizzle with balsamic vinaigrette and toss gently.
3. **Serve:**
    - Enjoy as a refreshing side or light main dish.

Vegan Pad Thai with Tofu

Ingredients

- 8 oz rice noodles
- 1 block firm tofu, cubed
- 2 tablespoons soy sauce
- 2 tablespoons peanut butter
- 1 tablespoon lime juice
- 1 tablespoon maple syrup
- 2 cups mixed vegetables (carrots, bell peppers, bean sprouts)
- Chopped peanuts and green onions for garnish

Instructions

1. **Cook Noodles:**
    - Prepare rice noodles according to package instructions; set aside.
2. **Sauté Tofu:**
    - In a skillet, sauté cubed tofu until golden brown. Remove and set aside.
3. **Prepare Sauce:**
    - In a bowl, mix soy sauce, peanut butter, lime juice, and maple syrup.
4. **Combine:**
    - In the same skillet, add mixed vegetables and sauté until tender. Stir in cooked noodles and sauce. Add tofu back in and mix well.
5. **Serve:**
    - Garnish with chopped peanuts and green onions.

Stuffed Acorn Squash with Quinoa

Ingredients

- 2 acorn squashes, halved and seeds removed
- 1 cup cooked quinoa
- 1/2 cup cranberries
- 1/2 cup walnuts, chopped
- 1 teaspoon cinnamon
- Salt and pepper to taste

Instructions

1. **Preheat Oven:**
   - Preheat your oven to 400°F (200°C). Place acorn squash halves cut-side down on a baking sheet and roast for 25-30 minutes until tender.
2. **Prepare Filling:**
   - In a bowl, mix cooked quinoa, cranberries, walnuts, cinnamon, salt, and pepper.
3. **Stuff Squash:**
   - Flip the roasted squash and fill each half with the quinoa mixture.
4. **Bake:**
   - Return to the oven for an additional 10-15 minutes.
5. **Serve:**
   - Enjoy warm!

Baked Falafel with Tahini Sauce

Ingredients

- 1 can (15 oz) chickpeas, rinsed and drained
- 1/4 cup parsley, chopped
- 1/4 cup onion, chopped
- 2 cloves garlic, minced
- 1 teaspoon cumin
- 1 teaspoon coriander
- Salt and pepper to taste
- 2 tablespoons flour
- Tahini sauce (for drizzling)

Instructions

1. **Preheat Oven:**
    - Preheat your oven to 375°F (190°C). Line a baking sheet with parchment paper.
2. **Blend Falafel Mixture:**
    - In a food processor, combine chickpeas, parsley, onion, garlic, cumin, coriander, salt, pepper, and flour. Blend until combined but not pureed.
3. **Form Falafel:**
    - Shape the mixture into small balls and place them on the baking sheet.
4. **Bake:**
    - Bake for 20-25 minutes, flipping halfway, until golden brown.
5. **Serve:**
    - Drizzle with tahini sauce and enjoy!

Zesty Lime Rice with Beans

Ingredients

- 1 cup brown rice
- 1 can (15 oz) black beans, rinsed and drained
- Juice of 2 limes
- 1 tablespoon olive oil
- 1/4 cup cilantro, chopped
- Salt and pepper to taste

Instructions

1. **Cook Rice:**
    - Cook brown rice according to package instructions; set aside.
2. **Combine Ingredients:**
    - In a large bowl, mix cooked rice, black beans, lime juice, olive oil, cilantro, salt, and pepper.
3. **Serve:**
    - Enjoy as a side or main dish!

Kale and Quinoa Salad

Ingredients

- 2 cups kale, chopped
- 1 cup cooked quinoa
- 1/2 cup cherry tomatoes, halved
- 1/4 cup almonds, sliced
- 2 tablespoons olive oil
- Juice of 1 lemon
- Salt and pepper to taste

Instructions

1. **Massage Kale:**
    - In a bowl, add chopped kale with a pinch of salt. Massage until wilted.
2. **Combine Ingredients:**
    - Add cooked quinoa, cherry tomatoes, and almonds.
3. **Dress Salad:**
    - Drizzle with olive oil and lemon juice. Season with salt and pepper.
4. **Serve:**
    - Enjoy chilled or at room temperature.

Coconut Rice with Mango

Ingredients

- 1 cup jasmine rice
- 1 can (14 oz) coconut milk
- 1/2 cup water
- 1 ripe mango, diced
- 2 tablespoons sugar (optional)
- Salt to taste

Instructions

1. **Cook Rice:**
    - In a pot, combine jasmine rice, coconut milk, water, sugar (if using), and salt. Bring to a boil.
2. **Simmer:**
    - Reduce heat, cover, and simmer for 15-20 minutes until rice is tender.
3. **Serve:**
    - Fluff rice with a fork and top with diced mango.

Enjoy your delicious meals!

Vegan Stuffed Cabbage Rolls

Ingredients

- 8 large cabbage leaves
- 1 cup cooked quinoa
- 1 can (15 oz) lentils, rinsed and drained
- 1 onion, diced
- 2 cloves garlic, minced
- 1 teaspoon Italian seasoning
- 1 can (15 oz) tomato sauce
- Salt and pepper to taste

Instructions

1. **Preheat Oven:**
   - Preheat your oven to 375°F (190°C).
2. **Prepare Filling:**
   - In a bowl, mix cooked quinoa, lentils, onion, garlic, Italian seasoning, salt, and pepper.
3. **Fill Cabbage Leaves:**
   - Blanch cabbage leaves in boiling water for 2-3 minutes until softened. Spoon filling into each leaf and roll tightly.
4. **Bake:**
   - Place rolls in a baking dish, cover with tomato sauce, and bake for 30 minutes.
5. **Serve:**
   - Enjoy warm!

Chickpea and Spinach Stew

Ingredients

- 1 can (15 oz) chickpeas, rinsed and drained
- 2 cups spinach, chopped
- 1 onion, diced
- 2 cloves garlic, minced
- 1 can (14 oz) diced tomatoes
- 1 teaspoon cumin
- Salt and pepper to taste

Instructions

1. **Sauté Vegetables:**
   - In a pot, sauté onion and garlic until translucent.
2. **Add Ingredients:**
   - Stir in chickpeas, spinach, diced tomatoes, cumin, salt, and pepper. Simmer for 15 minutes.
3. **Serve:**
   - Enjoy warm, optionally with rice or bread.

Grilled Eggplant with Tahini Drizzle

Ingredients

- 1 large eggplant, sliced into rounds
- 2 tablespoons olive oil
- Salt and pepper to taste
- 1/4 cup tahini
- Juice of 1 lemon
- Water (to thin, as needed)

Instructions

1. **Preheat Grill:**
    - Preheat your grill to medium-high heat.
2. **Prepare Eggplant:**
    - Brush eggplant slices with olive oil, and season with salt and pepper.
3. **Grill:**
    - Grill eggplant for 4-5 minutes on each side until tender and grill marks appear.
4. **Make Tahini Drizzle:**
    - In a bowl, whisk together tahini, lemon juice, and water to desired consistency.
5. **Serve:**
    - Drizzle tahini over grilled eggplant and enjoy!

Vegan Lentil Tacos

Ingredients

- 1 cup cooked lentils
- 1 tablespoon taco seasoning
- Corn or flour tortillas
- Toppings: diced tomatoes, avocado, lettuce, salsa

Instructions

1. **Heat Lentils:**
    - In a skillet, heat cooked lentils with taco seasoning until warm.
2. **Assemble Tacos:**
    - Spoon lentil mixture into tortillas and add desired toppings.
3. **Serve:**
    - Enjoy immediately!

Savory Oatmeal with Spinach and Avocado

Ingredients

- 1 cup rolled oats
- 2 cups vegetable broth
- 1 cup spinach, chopped
- 1 avocado, sliced
- Salt and pepper to taste

Instructions

1. **Cook Oats:**
    - In a pot, bring vegetable broth to a boil. Stir in rolled oats and reduce heat. Cook until creamy.
2. **Add Spinach:**
    - Stir in chopped spinach until wilted. Season with salt and pepper.
3. **Serve:**
    - Top with avocado slices and enjoy!

Cucumber and Avocado Sushi Rolls

Ingredients

- 1 cup sushi rice, cooked
- 4 nori sheets
- 1 cucumber, julienned
- 1 avocado, sliced
- Soy sauce (for serving)

Instructions

1. **Prepare Sushi:**
    - Lay a nori sheet on a bamboo mat. Spread a thin layer of sushi rice over the nori, leaving a border.
2. **Add Filling:**
    - Place cucumber and avocado in the center of the rice.
3. **Roll:**
    - Carefully roll the sushi tightly using the mat. Slice into pieces.
4. **Serve:**
    - Enjoy with soy sauce!

Maple Glazed Brussels Sprouts

Ingredients

- 1 lb Brussels sprouts, halved
- 2 tablespoons olive oil
- 2 tablespoons maple syrup
- Salt and pepper to taste

Instructions

1. **Preheat Oven:**
     - Preheat your oven to 400°F (200°C).
2. **Prepare Brussels Sprouts:**
     - Toss Brussels sprouts with olive oil, maple syrup, salt, and pepper.
3. **Bake:**
     - Spread on a baking sheet and roast for 20-25 minutes until caramelized.
4. **Serve:**
     - Enjoy warm!

Spicy Roasted Chickpeas

Ingredients

- 1 can (15 oz) chickpeas, rinsed and drained
- 2 tablespoons olive oil
- 1 teaspoon chili powder
- 1/2 teaspoon paprika
- Salt to taste

Instructions

1. **Preheat Oven:**
   - Preheat your oven to 400°F (200°C).
2. **Season Chickpeas:**
   - Toss chickpeas with olive oil, chili powder, paprika, and salt.
3. **Bake:**
   - Spread on a baking sheet and roast for 25-30 minutes until crispy.
4. **Serve:**
   - Enjoy as a snack or salad topping!

Enjoy your delicious meals!

Cauliflower Fried Rice

Ingredients

- 1 head cauliflower, grated into rice-like pieces
- 2 tablespoons olive oil
- 1 cup mixed vegetables (peas, carrots, bell peppers)
- 2 cloves garlic, minced
- 2 tablespoons soy sauce
- 2 green onions, chopped
- Salt and pepper to taste

Instructions

1. **Sauté Vegetables:**
    - In a large skillet, heat olive oil over medium heat. Add garlic and mixed vegetables, and sauté for 3-4 minutes until tender.
2. **Add Cauliflower:**
    - Stir in grated cauliflower and cook for another 5-7 minutes, stirring occasionally.
3. **Season:**
    - Add soy sauce, green onions, salt, and pepper. Mix well.
4. **Serve:**
    - Enjoy warm!

Miso Soup with Tofu and Seaweed

Ingredients

- 4 cups vegetable broth
- 3 tablespoons miso paste
- 1 cup firm tofu, cubed
- 1/4 cup dried seaweed (wakame)
- 2 green onions, sliced

Instructions

1. **Prepare Broth:**
    - In a pot, heat vegetable broth over medium heat.
2. **Mix Miso:**
    - In a small bowl, dissolve miso paste with a ladle of warm broth. Add back into the pot.
3. **Add Tofu and Seaweed:**
    - Stir in tofu and seaweed, cooking for 5 minutes until warmed.
4. **Serve:**
    - Garnish with green onions and enjoy!

Vegan Chocolate Avocado Pudding

Ingredients

- 2 ripe avocados
- 1/4 cup cocoa powder
- 1/4 cup maple syrup
- 1 teaspoon vanilla extract
- Pinch of salt

Instructions

1. **Blend Ingredients:**
    - In a food processor, combine avocados, cocoa powder, maple syrup, vanilla extract, and salt. Blend until smooth.
2. **Chill:**
    - Transfer to a bowl and refrigerate for at least 30 minutes.
3. **Serve:**
    - Enjoy chilled!

Berry and Spinach Smoothie Bowl

Ingredients

- 1 banana, frozen
- 1 cup mixed berries (fresh or frozen)
- 1 cup spinach
- 1/2 cup almond milk (or milk of choice)
- Toppings: sliced fruit, granola, seeds

Instructions

1. **Blend Smoothie:**
    - In a blender, combine banana, mixed berries, spinach, and almond milk. Blend until smooth.
2. **Serve:**
    - Pour into a bowl and top with your favorite toppings.

Curried Carrot and Apple Soup

Ingredients

- 4 cups carrots, chopped
- 1 apple, peeled and chopped
- 1 onion, diced
- 2 cloves garlic, minced
- 1 tablespoon curry powder
- 4 cups vegetable broth
- Salt and pepper to taste

Instructions

1. **Sauté Onion and Garlic:**
   - In a pot, sauté onion and garlic until soft. Stir in curry powder.
2. **Add Carrots and Apple:**
   - Add chopped carrots and apple. Pour in vegetable broth and bring to a boil.
3. **Simmer:**
   - Reduce heat and simmer for 20 minutes until carrots are tender.
4. **Blend:**
   - Use an immersion blender to puree until smooth. Season with salt and pepper.
5. **Serve:**
   - Enjoy warm!

Quinoa and Black Bean Burger

Ingredients

- 1 cup cooked quinoa
- 1 can (15 oz) black beans, rinsed and drained
- 1/4 cup breadcrumbs
- 1/4 cup onion, diced
- 1 tablespoon chili powder
- Salt and pepper to taste
- Olive oil (for cooking)

Instructions

1. **Mash Mixture:**
    - In a bowl, mash black beans. Stir in cooked quinoa, breadcrumbs, onion, chili powder, salt, and pepper.
2. **Form Patties:**
    - Shape mixture into patties.
3. **Cook:**
    - In a skillet, heat olive oil over medium heat. Cook patties for 4-5 minutes on each side until golden.
4. **Serve:**
    - Enjoy on buns or on their own!

Green Goddess Salad

Ingredients

- 4 cups mixed greens
- 1 avocado, diced
- 1 cup cucumber, sliced
- 1/2 cup peas (fresh or frozen)
- 1/4 cup fresh herbs (parsley, basil)
- Dressing: 1/4 cup tahini, juice of 1 lemon, water to thin

Instructions

1. **Prepare Dressing:**
    - In a bowl, whisk tahini, lemon juice, and enough water to reach desired consistency.
2. **Assemble Salad:**
    - In a large bowl, combine mixed greens, avocado, cucumber, and peas.
3. **Dress Salad:**
    - Drizzle with dressing and toss gently.
4. **Serve:**
    - Enjoy immediately!

Roasted Tomato and Basil Pasta

Ingredients

- 8 oz pasta (your choice)
- 2 cups cherry tomatoes, halved
- 2 tablespoons olive oil
- Salt and pepper to taste
- 1/4 cup fresh basil, chopped
- Parmesan cheese (optional)

Instructions

1. **Preheat Oven:**
   - Preheat your oven to 400°F (200°C). Toss cherry tomatoes with olive oil, salt, and pepper. Spread on a baking sheet.
2. **Roast Tomatoes:**
   - Roast for 20-25 minutes until caramelized.
3. **Cook Pasta:**
   - Meanwhile, cook pasta according to package instructions; drain.
4. **Combine:**
   - Toss cooked pasta with roasted tomatoes and fresh basil. Add cheese if desired.
5. **Serve:**
   - Enjoy warm!

Enjoy your delicious meals!

Plant-Based Sushi with Vegetables

Ingredients

- 2 cups sushi rice, cooked
- 4 nori sheets
- 1 cucumber, julienned
- 1 carrot, julienned
- 1 avocado, sliced
- 1 red bell pepper, sliced
- Soy sauce (for dipping)

Instructions

1. **Prepare Sushi:**
    - Lay a nori sheet on a bamboo mat. Spread a thin layer of sushi rice over the nori, leaving a border at the top.
2. **Add Vegetables:**
    - Place cucumber, carrot, avocado, and bell pepper in the center of the rice.
3. **Roll:**
    - Carefully roll the sushi tightly using the mat. Seal the edge with a bit of water.
4. **Slice:**
    - Slice into bite-sized pieces and serve with soy sauce.

Chocolate Chia Seed Energy Bites

Ingredients

- 1 cup oats
- 1/4 cup chia seeds
- 1/4 cup nut butter (peanut or almond)
- 1/4 cup maple syrup
- 1/4 cup cocoa powder
- 1/4 cup dark chocolate chips (optional)

Instructions

1. **Mix Ingredients:**
   - In a bowl, combine oats, chia seeds, nut butter, maple syrup, cocoa powder, and chocolate chips. Mix until well combined.
2. **Chill Mixture:**
   - Refrigerate for about 30 minutes to firm up.
3. **Form Bites:**
   - Once chilled, scoop out small portions and roll into balls.
4. **Store:**
   - Keep in the refrigerator in an airtight container for up to a week. Enjoy as a snack!

www.ingramcontent.com/pod-product-compliance
Lightning Source LLC
LaVergne TN
LVHW081343060526
838201LV00055B/2820